Welcome to the

Shelly Shines
Activity Book

Teacher's Guide

Author
Rochelle Forrest Hankins

Illustrator Terre Britton

ShellyShines™ BOOKS

Text Copyright © 2018 by Rochelle Forrest Hankins
Published by ShellyShines™ Books
9134 Forest Willow Dr.
Indianapolis, IN 46234

Printed in the United States of America

First Printing, 2018
ISBN 978-0-9993131-3-8

www.ShellyShines.com
www.rochelleforrest.com
www.tummiesmindsspirits.com

Illustration Copyright © 2018 by Terre Britton
Produced by Terrabyte Graphics
www.tbytegraphics.com

terrabyte graphics

Table of Contents

Notes

The story of how I discovered my inner light was told in the book *Shelly and the Circle of Light.*

Did you read it?

That book tells all about a journey I went on to learn about my purpose and about myself.

On my journey, I met amazing new friends and learned some very important lessons.

Are you ready to go on your own adventure?

Do you want to discover your inner light?

Would you like to help the world?

Come on, let's go!

Welcome to the Shelly Shines Activity Book

Teacher's Guide

The **Shelly Shines Activity Book** should be used after reading **Shelly and the Circle of Light**, which will introduce the concept of finding your own light, meaning each person should find how they can best serve through joy. Each character will appear in the Activity Book and guide the lessons.

Notes

In this adventure book, you will meet some of my friends from Shelly and the Circle of Light.

I hope you are excited to meet them.

Together, we will share **ten important lessons** with you. They will help you discover your inner light, too!

There are also a lot of **fun things** for you to do along the way...

There are places for you to write, draw, and color in the book.

And there are fun activities to do.

When you see one of these symbols on the next page, it means there is an activity to enjoy.

The Shelly Concept

The Shelly concept goes beyond the children's story. She endeavors to teach each child, and by extension the adults involved, to think beyond themselves and to see the world as a place of joy, service, and abundance.

Notes

My Symbols

 Aha!
Write or draw your ideas.

 Tuck-in!
A bedtime activity.

 Switch-on!
Think a bright thought.

 Team up!
Get help from your parent or guardian.

 Speak-up!
Ask questions.

 Connect!
Meet other kids.

 Share!
Give to someone else.

 Feel!
Listen to you heart.

Lesson #1
– from Shelly the Lightning Bug

Hello again. It's me, Shelly.

Introduction

Each lesson has a series of activities designed not only to explain the concepts but to foster cooperation and creativity. Please highlight each of the symbols and encourage the children to complete each exercise and share with the group.

Each lesson ends with a place for children to write notes about what they have learned and experienced. Encourage them to fill these spaces in to share with their families.

Work through each lesson and activity. Depending on the length of session and the age of the children each lesson can span 2-3 sessions. Teachers should encourage discussion of concepts and design activities that are appropriate to their particular group of children.

When available, bringing in locally gifted people community members is encouraged.

Suggestions for overarching class projects are a picture book showing progress, or creating an adventure bulletin board.

This adventure book ends with the Joy Project where students are encouraged to create a community service project. Teachers should work with local officials to determine what is possible and advisable in their areas, and when possible get parental involvement. Consider partnering with other classes or organizations, or obtaining invitations for the children to participate in a larger community activity already in progress.

Notes

Listen carefully. I want to share a special secret with you.

I am going to tell you where **joy** comes from.

★ **What is joy? It is happiness!** ★

The very best kind of happiness!

Do you want to know where it comes from?

It comes from inside you! **It's true!**

I discovered what it means to be **joyful** when I learned how I am

unique and how to **share** my special gifts with the world.

We are all the same in many ways, and we are also very different.

We are each unique in special ways ... including you!

I'm a lightning bug! What are you?

You may not think you are special or unique, but I know that you are.

You see, God has given every one of us three things that we can share with others:

Write them down in the space provided.

My Talents:

Write them down in the space provided.

My Treasures:

.•❤ Time, Talent and Treasure! ❤•.

When you use your time to **share** your **unique** talents and treasures, you will experience joy inside!

? What are your unique talents?

Maybe you have a great smile, or you give terrific hugs. Perhaps you can sing well or run fast.

Can you make people laugh?

What else are you talented at?

How many things can you think of?

? What special treasures do you have?

What things do you have that are important to you that you can share? Do you have toys, candy, jokes, or money? Maybe a pet or a good book?

Make a list of treasures that you could share with others.

If you get stuck for ideas, ask your family or friends to help you!

Okay, here is the best part. Pick one talent or one treasure that you are willing to share.

Lesson 1: Time, Talent, and Treasure

Engage: Shelly teaches us **self-awareness**.

Ask the children to highlight their unique talents and encourage positive awareness in others. Promote brainstorming about qualities that are intangible: a sister who always knows when you need a hug; a brother who understands your question, even when you're vague; a friend who keeps you excited about going to school by singing at the bus stop. Offer your suggestions.

Discuss: Open a discussion about what inspires each child to feel special. Our culture often focuses on failures and negative comparison to others. Encourage the children to appreciate their individuality without comparison. The conclusion should be that there is no one way to feel special or to find joy, and we should urge each other to find those special opportunities. All chances for joy are welcome and essential.

Encourage: When discussing treasures, be sure to expand on the idea that treasures aren't always material *things,* and they can be shared without giving *things* away: like playing together with a pet or a toy, or enjoying playing a game together. Generosity should not be equated with loss but with joy.

Focus: Joy, Uniqueness, and Sharing

Notes

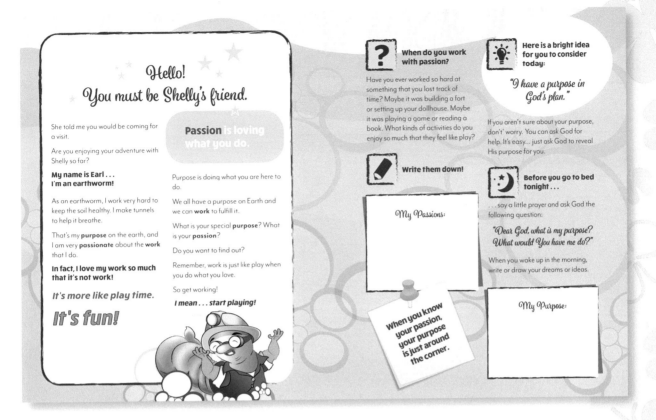

Lesson 2: Purpose and Passion

Engage: Earl teaches **Lesson 2**. His focus is **work ethic**.

Engage children in a discussion of those in their lives who *live* their passion. A coach, mom, or teacher? Maybe a best friend? Encourage specific examples. Offer suggestions from age- and location-specific media.

Discuss: Ask each child what he or she is passionate about, and to describe why. Also, part of the learning process is not only learning what you like but learning what you don't.

Open a discussion about activities they have not enjoyed and if they had a positive or negative learning experience.

Encourage: Earl loves to dig in the dirt, but Shelly doesn't. It is important to encourage children to learn from activities they don't enjoy.

Focus: Working With Purpose And Passion

Notes

Lesson 3: Cooperation and Teamwork

Engage: Wesley the Ant teaches about **working together**.

Children can easily see this principle if they watch an ant hill. Explain, through the example of ants, the ability to achieve more in a cohesive group than singly. What activities can they think of that are more effective when done by a group?

Discuss: Ask the children to discuss what teams they are part of, starting with your group, then family, school, church, sports, and so on.

Ask what role each child plays on one of their teams?

Refer to **Lesson 1** and ask them to share what talents they bring to their team.

Ask them to give examples of their team accomplishments that could not have been reached by themselves.

Ask if they would like to be part of other teams.

Encourage: Remind them that what they give to a team is as important as anything they might receive from participating.

Focus: Teamwork, Cooperation And Family

Notes

We met Shelly when she was searching for her purpose.

What a lovely little lightning bug she is!

Shelly tells us that you are exploring your own passion and purpose, too!

Good for you!

Here is a little secret that will help you on your adventure:

As flowers, one of the *treasures* we share with the world is our **beauty**.

Aren't flowers beautiful? It's just who we are!

We fulfill our purpose simply by **being** who we are...and so can you!

Who you are is beautiful, too! So just be yourself!

You can also look for the beauty in others and appreciate who they are.

We all have beauty to share.

Remember, <u>real beauty</u> is <u>being</u> who you are, not who someone else thinks you should be.

Who do you want to be?

Make a list of the beauty you see in others.

Maybe you like someone's smile, or their eyes, or how generous they are. Perhaps you like the way someone speaks, or how they always say nice things to others. Include pets, too! Maybe your dog or cat is beautiful because they are friendly and loving. How many things can you think of? Write them down on the next page!

(Remember, boys and girls can both be beautiful! **Beauty is for everyone**.)

Here is a bright idea for today:

"Not everyone can see their own beauty. Sometimes they need reminders from someone like me!"

Share! Give to someone else.

Remind someone you care for about their beauty. Tell them:

"The beauty I see in you is _____."

Fill in the blank with whatever is beautiful about them.

How does that feel?

How did they respond?

Ask your parents:

Ask your parent or guardian to tell you about the beauty they see in you!

Lesson 4: Beauty

Engage: The Roses reveal that there are **different aspects of beauty**. All flowers are pretty, but they don't look or smell the same.

Our society is obsessed with narrow views of beauty, usually physical traits and, often, distorted features, such as a too-thin female body, perfect skin, the shiniest hair, or a steroid-enhanced muscular male physique.

Discuss: Beauty is all around us and can be in something as simple and universally accessible as a smile, or in a pretty voice that makes you feel special.

Encourage: A child who is unhappy, or in a bad place emotionally, often can't see his or her own beauty, or the beauty in others. Ask them to discuss their negative feelings and solutions to combat them.

Suggest that each child see themselves through the eyes of love, rather than an external social role model, and encourage them to appreciate their own special beauty.

Then, ask them to offer insights into the beauty of their classmates—re-framing a situation often lets us see things from a different perspective.

Focus: Beauty And Being Yourself

Notes

You might have seen me floating on the soft breeze in the forest, just like Shelly did when I first met her.

Although Shelly and I only spoke for a moment that day, she was quickly struck by **inspiration**.

Inspiration is when you are moved by Spirit or God.

Through inspiration, Shelly was **motivated** to discover her talents.

Motivation is being eager to do something.

Very soon, Shelly discovered that she could fly!

Do you see how I helped Shelly?

Just by being myself and living my own purpose, I **inspired** Shelly and she was **motivated** to discover her special gift!

We can all be inspired by others. And we can inspire others, too! Even you!

You can motivate and inspire others through your choices and actions.

Who do you want to inspire?

What inspires you?

 Speak up!

When do you feel moved by Spirit and motivated to do something? What kinds of actions are the most inspiring to you?

 Imagine!

Lie on your belly and lift our arms and legs off the ground. Pretend you are flying.

How does it feel?

Imagine you can fly anywhere and do anything right now. Where would you go? What would you do? Who could you help?

 Write down your vision.

Write down your vision or draw a picture of what you feel inspired to do!

 Here is a bright idea for today:

"I can inspire others with my choices and behavior."

 Ask your parents:

Find an inspiring video or movie to watch with your family. Ask your parents to help you pick one.

Lesson 5: Inspiration and Motivation

Engage: Bella the Butterfly teaches us about **transformation**.

Point out that inspiration is already inside each of us and that one way for a child to see what inspires them is to think about how they like to play. Then expand on that to see how it might help them help others. Encourage a group discussion.

Discuss: Motivation is the unpacking of our inspiration and using it to make things happen. *How* would your kids like to help people?

Be true to yourself. Not everyone is packed with the same stuff inside. Discuss how various sorts of inspiration could come together to make something bigger happen.

Discussion option: Are you in the parade, watching the parade, or did you not notice the parade? Do you want to lead the parade? What is your parade about?

Encourage: Help each child to figure out their place in the parade and what the best path might be for them to reach that goal.

Focus: Inspiration And Motivation

Notes

How are you doing with discovering your passion and your purpose?

I am happy to see you are still learning how to use your time, talent and treasures wisely. *Good for you!*

Do you want to know something else that will help you figure it out?

Let me tell you about connection.

I've spent many years working the soil, and I know that we are all connected on this planet!

We've only got one home...Earth! We need the Earth to provide our food, shelter, clothing and more!

Because we are all connected, we also need to learn about **sharing** and **caring**.

Caring is being considerate of others.

It means thinking about other people, animals, insects and everyone who lives on the Earth.

Sharing is being generous and helping others get what they need.

When you care about others, sharing is natural.

When you discover your **connections** to others, you will naturally want to **care** and **share**.

Who can you care for?

Who can you help to get what they need?

Explore the Earth

With the help of an adult, find a globe or a map of the Earth.

Now explore the world!

Notice how small it is in your hands. As you discover the Earth, look at the names of some other countries.

Are there countries you have never heard of?

Pick one to explore! Pick a country you didn't know about before. Do you think there might be kids your age who live in that country? **There are!**

Here is a bright idea for today:

"I share because I care."

Remember: We are all connected!

Connect with other kids

With the help of an adult, use a computer to meet a child your age in that country. Get to know them. Make friends. Ask questions about what's important to them. Is there something you can share with the people you meet?

Before you go to bed tonight . . .

In what ways are you connected to kids in that country? Use your imagination!

Lesson 6: Caring and Connection

Engage: Earl teaches us about **connection** and the importance of **caring and sharing**.

The more we know about others, the more they become part of our expanded tribe, and the more we are able to care for them. This lesson hopes to shift perspective from "me" to "we".

The activities are designed to find other kids around the world. If this is not feasible, teachers may recommend finding another group in your community who could connect with your students.

Discuss: In random drawings, pair up kids from different classes, church groups, or sports. Invite the other group to an activity and as a group activity create a list of "getting to know you" questions to share with their new friends. When they return to class, encourage each child to share new things he or she learned from their connections.

Encourage: This lesson lends itself particularly well to community projects. Start discussions moving toward **The Joy Project** after **Lesson 10**.

Focus: Connection, Sharing And Caring

Notes

Lesson 7: Commitment and Dedication

Engage: Wesley talks about being **willing to work** for things that are important.

Commitment is the drive to keep going even when it's hard, or you don't *feel* like it. **Dedication** is getting up and doing the same thing tomorrow.

Both sports and good grades are excellent frameworks for these concepts.

Ask a local celebrity to give a presentation on commitment and dedication to their sport. **Many sports figures have given interviews which are** available online. Teenagers prominent in the area can also be excellent speakers for this topic.

Discuss: Find out which sports or musical instruments they play. Are they team sports? Are they part of a band? Ask them to name other activities that require commitment and dedication?

Encourage: Urge the children to follow through with commitments— even their least favorite—then they can choose something else. Teach them to be grateful for all lessons learned, including their least favorite or *failures*. We all need to learn from mistakes.

Focus: Commitment And Dedication

Notes

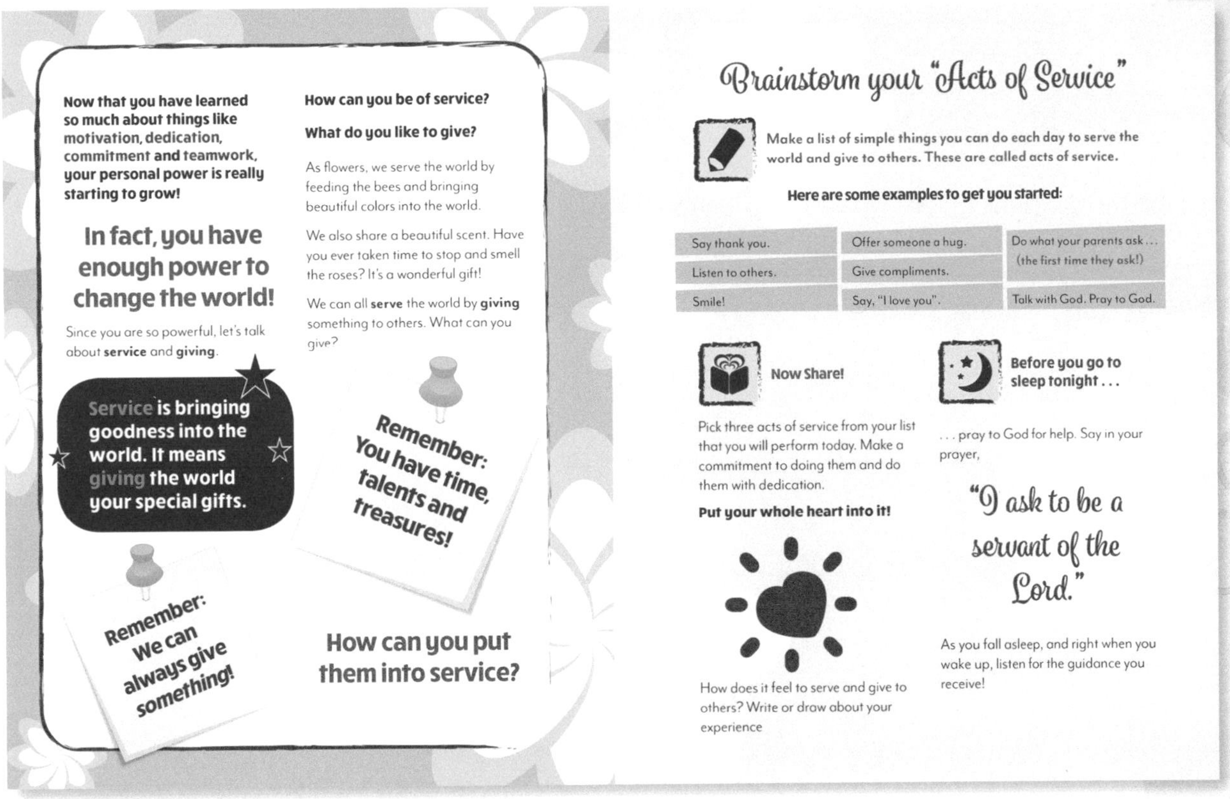
Now that you have learned so much about things like motivation, dedication, commitment and teamwork, your personal power is really starting to grow!

In fact, you have enough power to change the world!

Since you are so powerful, let's talk about **service** and **giving**.

Service is bringing goodness into the world. It means giving the world your special gifts.

Remember: We can always give something!

How can you be of service?

What do you like to give?

As flowers, we serve the world by feeding the bees and bringing beautiful colors into the world.

We also share a beautiful scent. Have you ever taken time to stop and smell the roses? It's a wonderful gift!

We can all **serve** the world by **giving** something to others. What can you give?

Remember: You have time, talents and treasures!

How can you put them into service?

Brainstorm your "Acts of Service"

Make a list of simple things you can do each day to serve the world and give to others. These are called acts of service.

Here are some examples to get you started:

Say thank you.	Offer someone a hug.	Do what your parents ask... (the first time they ask!)
Listen to others.	Give compliments.	
Smile!	Say, "I love you".	Talk with God. Pray to God.

Now Share!

Pick three acts of service from your list that you will perform today. Make a commitment to doing them and do them with dedication.

Put your whole heart into it!

How does it feel to serve and give to others? Write or draw about your experience

Before you go to sleep tonight...

... pray to God for help. Say in your prayer,

"I ask to be a servant of the Lord."

As you fall asleep, and right when you wake up, listen for the guidance you receive!

Lesson 8: Service and Giving

Engage: The Roses teach us that we **can change the world** if we are willing to put in the effort, one small thing at a time.

Remind the children that giving of their talents and treasures is as essential as adults serving as teachers and firemen.

Discuss: Service and **giving** are important, but taking care of ourselves is also important. You can't serve from an empty pitcher! Signs of an empty pitcher can be being tired or grumpy.

Lead a conversation about other signs you may be giving too much and when to replenish yourself. How do people replenish themselves?

Explain that it's okay to say *no* sometimes, and not every kind of sharing will make everyone feel good. You don't have to give everything to everyone.

Encourage: Ask the children to explore what kinds of service they like to give. What are simple acts that can be done every day for a low personal cost? Picking up trash, smiling, giving compliments, doing chores at home without being asked. Even just asking to help can be an act of giving.

Notes

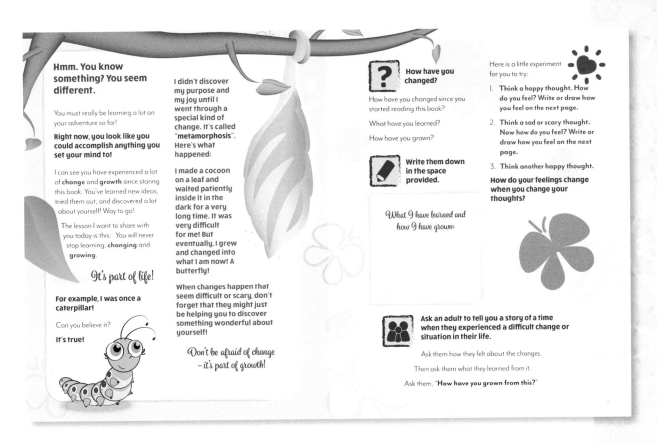

Hmm. You know something? You seem different.

You must really be learning a lot on your adventure so far!

Right now, you look like you could accomplish anything you set your mind to!

I can see you have experienced a lot of **change** and **growth** since staring this book. You've learned new ideas, tried them out, and discovered a lot about yourself! Way to go!

The lesson I want to share with you today is this: You will never stop learning, **changing** and **growing**.

It's part of life!

For example, I was once a caterpillar!

Can you believe it?

It's true!

I didn't discover my purpose and my joy until I went through a special kind of change. It's called "metamorphosis". Here's what happened:

I made a cocoon on a leaf and waited patiently inside it in the dark for a very long time. It was very difficult for me! But eventually, I grew and changed into what I am now! A butterfly!

When changes happen that seem difficult or scary, don't forget that they might just be helping you to discover something wonderful about yourself!

Don't be afraid of change – it's part of growth!

? How have you changed?

How have you changed since you started reading this book?

What have you learned?

How have you grown?

✏ Write them down in the space provided.

What I have learned and how I have grown:

👥 Ask an adult to tell you a story of a time when they experienced a difficult change or situation in their life.

Ask them how they felt about the changes.

Then ask them what they learned from it.

Ask them, "**How have you grown from this?**"

Here is a little experiment for you to try:

1. **Think a happy thought. How do you feel? Write or draw how you feel on the next page.**

2. **Think a sad or scary thought. Now how do you feel? Write or draw how you feel on the next page.**

3. **Think another happy thought.**

How do your feelings change when you change your thoughts?

Lesson 9: Change and Growth

Engage: Bella explains about her **metamorphosis**.

If possible, collaborate with a science or nature-oriented group. Seek documentation or examples of butterfly metamorphosis.

Discuss: If age appropriate, include a discussion of human metamorphosis from child to adult.

Explain that change doesn't happen quickly, most of the time. We won't always get things right the first time. We might need a teacher before we can learn something. We might not be very good, at first. These experiences are all normal. When you learn new things, you won't always get it right the first time. Discuss the idea "When you fall, fall forward."

It can be difficult when you change, and others around you change at a different rate. Some friends might change faster or slower. It's ok to change and make new friends who share those changes.

Encourage: Help refresh their memory of things they have learned that took time and effort.

Notes

When you have the courage to **explore**, you will **discover** amazing things.

You will learn about yourself, uncover your special gifts (like time, talent and treasure) and you will be excited to share them with the world.

Making those discoveries will help you experience...Joy!

And what is Joy?

The very best kind happiness!

(Remember: It's inside of you!)

Speaking of adventure ... are you ready for the final adventure in this book?

Do you want to do something amazing?

Come on, let's go!

Today I learned about:
EXPLORATION and DISCOVERY

As you continue your journey to explore and discover who you are, you will also meet amazing people along the way. . . just like my friends! They will help you in your adventure.

The Joy Project

You are a wonderful person. Thank you for being my friend! I believe in you.

You really have a lot to offer. You have so much to give!

Very soon, I will invite you to start a "**Joy Project**" to help you discover just how much you can give.

Your project will bring the very best kind of happiness to you and others. It will help you experience all the lessons you learned in this book.

I'm very excited for you. A **Joy Project** is a lot of fun.

It is going to take some effort, but I know you can do it!

But first, let me give you some encouragement by reminding you how much you've learned in this book.

Lesson 10: Exploration

Engage: Shelly teaches that **exploration** and **discovery** lead to joy, and joy comes from within.

We are all packed perfectly for our jobs here, but sometimes we need help to unpack what is inside us. Who do you want on your team? Whose team do you want to be on?

Discuss: We learn by trying new things. Exploration and discovery is easier with excited and encouraging people. Negative or grumpy people can make an adventure disappointing or scary. Ask them how they would try help grumpy team-members.

Promote new perspectives: Finishing something doesn't have to mean it's over; it can be the start of something else. It's all how you look at things.

Think about the things they tried that they did and didn't like, and why? Was it the people? Too much, not enough activity? What did they learn? What do the students want to try? Where would they like to travel?

Encourage: Joy is good for everyone. Teach children to celebrate all things: both successes and failures because they help us discover who we are, and who we will become.

Focus: Exploration And Discovery

Notes

Here are the ten lessons my friends and I shared with you:

1. We all have unique gifts. God gives us time, talent and treasure to share with others.

2. We all have a purpose in God's plan. You can follow your passion to find your purpose.

3. We all can have a team to help us. Cooperation is working together as a team.

4. We all are beautiful. Beauty is simply being who you are.

5. We all can inspire and motivate others. Your choices and actions are important.

6. We all are connected to the Earth and each other. Caring and sharing are natural when you're connected to others.

7. We all get to choose what's really important to us. Commitment and dedication help us to create what is important.

8. We all can be of service by giving to others. Even simple acts of service are powerful.

9. We all will change and grow over time. Change can be scary, but it's part of growing.

10. We all are on the adventure of a lifetime. Exploring and discovering will help you experience Joy!

Wow, you've learned so much!

Are you ready to start your Joy Project?

Let's do it!

My Joy Project

A Joy Project is something you do to help the world. It will also help you experience Joy! My friends and I think you can help make this world a better place.

We invite you to pick a Joy Project to help make a difference.

Here are some examples of what a Joy Project might be:

- Organize a "Clean up the Neighborhood Day" and go out with friends and neighbors to pick up litter and make the neighborhood look nice.

- Spend an afternoon with senior citizens.

- Serve meals to the homeless at a food shelter.

- Raise money for a good cause.

- Write a letter to a local politician asking them to help solve a problem in your city or country.

- Send clothing or school supplies to kids in countries where they don't have enough.

- Help a village in another country by raising money to provide them with housing, clean water, or medicine.

- Make a website or a video to raise awareness about something you care about.

- Start your own charity to help other kids.

There are **no limits** to what you can dream up or how much you can accomplish.

Just follow your heart!

Review

Encourage a discussion about each lesson and what the children primarily took from them. Which were their favorites? How can they share them with their friends and family?

Brainstorm about potential community projects. It is best to be pre-prepared with several options that have been vetted by supervisors, parents, or other appropriate local leaders.

Focus: Resourcefulness and Commitment

Notes

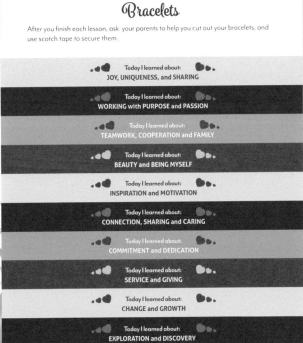

Bracelets

After you finish each lesson, ask your parents to help you cut out your bracelets, and use scotch tape to secure them.

Today I learned about:
JOY, UNIQUENESS, and SHARING

Today I learned about:
WORKING with PURPOSE and PASSION

Today I learned about:
TEAMWORK, COOPERATION and FAMILY

Today I learned about:
BEAUTY and BEING MYSELF

Today I learned about:
INSPIRATION and MOTIVATION

Today I learned about:
CONNECTION, SHARING and CARING

Today I learned about:
COMMITMENT and DEDICATION

Today I learned about:
SERVICE and GIVING

Today I learned about:
CHANGE and GROWTH

Today I learned about:
EXPLORATION and DISCOVERY

The Bracelets

On the very last day of the project, have paper copies of the bracelets available for children to offer each other. Be prepared with glue or tape.

To ensure all students receive bracelets, please visit our website: **www.shellyshines.com**, to download a free, printable, color PDF of all the bracelets.

Focus: Joyful Reminders!

Notes

Made in the USA
Columbia, SC
22 February 2024

32100792R00020